Awakening the Optimal Leader

Accelerate the Realization of Your Vision as an Awakened Organization

I0101901

Awakening the Optimal Leader

Accelerate the Realization of Your Vision
as an Awakened Organization

Mark Hattas

and the Rookha Group team

Rookha
publications

ISBN: 978-0-9994815-0-9

Within you is your Optimal Being® state of living. It is a state of living as the essence of who you are, as the perfect love from which you come. Leaders who lead from this state have awakened the Optimal Leader in them.

Acknowledgments

Thank you to God, family, friends, and all who inspire healthy, happy, fulfilling lives. Thank you to my mother, father and sisters. I grew up in a blessed family and appreciate you all. Thank you to my wife, Liz, a woman who has courage, love, compassion and strength, and who has embraced me when I was flying high and when I hit rock bottom. You are a wonderful woman, wife, mother, and human being! To our children, John, Charlie, David, Henry, and Sophie, your mom and I see you as love, perfectly created by the Creator, and a gift we are forever grateful for.

Thank you to Rookha Group, Inc. and all who are working on its behalf and on behalf of its customers. Many thanks to Rex (co-founder) and Mitzi Montague-Bauer, Breaha (co-founder) and Zach Wallin, Dr. Paul Repicky (partner), Dr. Timothy Hayes (expert collaborator), Dr. Michael (dedicated practitioner and teacher) and Jeanie Ryce, and Dave (coach) and Cathy Austin and family, for all of your many contributions to this story.

Thank you also to the organizations, leaders, and mentors whom I have learned from at CEO Space International, The Junto Institute, Vistage International, Powerful U, YPO, i.c. stars, Geneca, Corporate Strategies & Solutions, Inc., Thinking for Success, Inc., The Wright Foundation, GE Healthcare, and the many other companies I contributed to and learned from early in my career.

Special thanks to Leon Smith Publishing, who supplied a fabulous team for this project. I am so thankful to know its founder, Keith Leon and his wife, Maura, who have transformed publishing business books to be less work and more fun.

Extra special thanks to the many practitioners who supported my health and well-being from bipolar I disorder to healthy, a true-life miracle transformation that we hope will influence many as they navigate their way to optimal mental health and their optimal life. For those interested, check out Journey's Dream and discover a mental health resource portal (www. journeysdream.org).

Lastly, many thanks to my spiritual mentor and teacher since birth, Jesus. I love that I know you and appreciate all that my life has become with you in it.

Contents

PART 2

Preface

With great humility, I share this book with you, a fellow leader seeking to support the betterment of yourself and those you lead. A remarkable thread of events in my life revealed a set of principles and practices to live an optimal life. Once I experienced the effects of these, I made a commitment to share them with others, so they too can discover their path to living their optimal life. Doing so significantly improves one's leadership capabilities and, more, much more!!!

There are three important things to know before delving into the main story:

First, I built and sold a very successful tech company. So, I know what it is like to be in your shoes.

Second, after selling, I went through a life change that was rather disruptive. You will read about it in the Prologue. The key message is that adversity will come into all of our lives. True leaders find paths through adversity, learn from it, and appreciate its gifts. I have done this and have some wisdom to share.

Third, we all have within us an optimal being, and when we live as this optimal being, we know who we are. When we know who we are, our #1 priority is to maintain that presence of being above everything of the world. It is the first step to living as an optimal leader. The following story illustrates this and shares insights about how you too can live as your optimal being consistently.

The following book was first audio recorded during one 90-minute sitting. It was a remarkable journey to have that occur. It began when our 9-year-old son asked me to tell him a bedtime story in October of 2015. Night after night, this continued until one night, a very new experience transpired.

That night, I heard an inner voice speak, "Mark, don't tell him a story; allow the story to come." It was like a wise friend arriving to teach me something important, something that would change the trajectory of my life. I listened, took a deep breath and my mouth began to move. Words came. They were incredible. It was fresh and good. It felt as if the story was being told by someone else and yet it was coming through me. I felt at peace and was in awe. The story that flowed was far better than any I had previously shared. Wanting to know if Henry noticed the difference, I asked, "What did you think of that?"

As if he knew something was happening in me, he gave me a thumbs up and said, "That was really good, Dad." After a pause, he continued, "It's just going to get better. I know you're just learning."

He was right. The intuitive guidance that came so clearly that night led to more stories, and eventually this book was effortlessly written. I've come to know this inner voice as my own, and I've come to trust this intuition.

Everyone has the potential for refined intuitive skills. They come into our active possession and are strengthened when we are aligned with our Optimal Being, love, the essence of who we are. Anything in the way of this truth must fall away or be corrected for our intuitive skills to manifest.

Imagine leading with all your intuitive gifts online and active 100% of the time. The leaders of tomorrow will all have this, just as every computer today has access to the internet. A computer is severely limited without the internet just as a human is severely limited when out of alignment with their Optimal Being.

Will you activate your intuitive guidance and use all your faculties to live a life that is optimal for you? Will you do this and join the many who are Awakening the Optimal Leader in them?

PART 1

PROLOGUE

The following story is true. It begins that way anyway. Then it leaps in time to the year 2037.

It tells the story of two companies, one using the principles of optimal living and one struggling in contrast; at least before the two meet. The premise, in the year 2037, is that Rookha Group, Inc., an actual company, has achieved its mission of directly and indirectly influencing millions of people living their optimal lives, something they believe is possible for all.

The following back story leads up to the 2016 legal formation of Rookha Group. My name is Mark Hattas. I am one of the founders of Rookha Group, supporting people living their best lives as they lead in their homes, communities, and organizations, creating environments ripe for thriving. You may wonder why I am so passionate about this. It is because I experienced, firsthand, what it is like to live stressed, overwhelmed, fearful, dysfunctional and out of alignment.

We begin on Saturday, September 10, 2011. It was exactly nine months following the sale of my interest in Geneca, a software business I helped start and build between 1998 and 2010. We finished 2010 with about $20M in sales and 150 people in our stellar workforce.

After much drama that Saturday, Liz, my wife (and mother of our five children), called the paramedics. It had been nearly a week of me exhibiting unusual behavior. Neither of us understood the experience or how it would influence our lives. Still, we were both aware something strange was happening: The miracle of my back healing, conversations with spirits, a wall moved, no eating for days on end. Yes, something strange was definitely at play. While Liz had grown more and more afraid that it would end with me hurting me, I imagined this was what it would be like to be on an LSD trip. I had never actually done drugs, so I couldn't be sure. An intervention mid-day with family, friends, and our parish Priest looked to be the answer she was hoping for, but they left as I agreed to take myself to the mental hospital. I didn't go. Later that night, I was locked in the bathroom, growling like a lion. Liz had had enough. She finally called the paramedics. Things had gone too far.

After a visit to the ER and transfer to the Linden Oaks Behavioral Health facility, a much-needed night's sleep came, aided by a potent antipsychotic medication. A Doctor soon diagnosed me with Bipolar I Disorder. It was a frightening time. Our children were young, and Liz watched her stability, her rock, go off the deep end. Meanwhile, I hated losing what I had, those "superhuman" abilities, as the medicine knocked me back to "normal." It was like going

100 mph on a mental superhighway and screeching to a crawl during one of Chicago's bearish rush hours. I tried to understand what happened to me but only had questions and few, if any, answers. I was genuinely confused about what actually occurred. Everything was different. Trust in me was lost. Freedoms appeared to be stripped away, and I felt empty, helpless, and rejected. It didn't cross my mind that the doctor was able to help me. After all, upon my hospital discharge, he told me I would never get well, and I would likely be on medication for the rest of my life, not an inspiring message.

This same doctor asked me not to work for six months, yet I was on stage speaking at a TEDx Naperville event within six weeks. Soon after starting, I had an out of body experience, quite literally watching my body give this talk from off stage. I could see my lips moving but heard no sound. Fascination shifted to curiosity. Instantly, upon asking, *How is this happening?* My awareness shifted back into my body. The words ceased. I had no idea where I was in the talk and stood silent for many — what felt like thirty or so — seconds.

The audience began shifting, and I could almost hear them saying, "Come on, Mark, you can do it." The pause was edited in the posted talk, but the live version was filled with discomfort for me and the audience. Did I regain composure? Not really, not the way I would have liked. Today, I would tell the audience what might have been happening, or at least my experience of it. But on that day, I was determined to deliver that talk and was newer to speaking, so I didn't even consider a real-time adjustment of that magnitude.

Feeling devastated and embarrassed was how I left the stage. However, multiple people asked if I had done it on purpose, perceiving it as a positive, powerful pause. Though some may think an out of body experience would be cool, and it was for a moment, I felt out of control. After all, if I was not in my body, how was it moving about? What would it do without me? My fear: I might hurt someone. A flood of memories surfaced of times when I had hurt people physically or emotionally. They were few but very real and raw. I wanted to be in control and conscious at all times. Hercules killing his wife and family without a memory of it was my anchor of how important it was to stay vigilant.

Soon after, I sat in bed and prayed, "God, if there is a way to heal this, please show me the way." Instantly, my hand lifted from its position and reached for a book on the side of our bed. I had a dozen or so stacked up on the floor. It was like something came online in me, moved my hand, grabbed a book, and opened up to a chapter for me to read.

It was a book about St. Teresa of Avila. The chapter

I opened to described her mystical experiences that were somewhat like mine. Inspired hope arose in me. I laughed and realized at that moment I could look at this differently and actually get well.

Soon after, I felt an urge to call the author of another book, Why Is This Happening to Me . . . Again? by Dr. Michael Ryce. He called me back and became the first person to support my belief that I could get well. He invited me to join him at a 9-day healing intensive he was hosting in April of 2012. There was no way I thought Liz would approve. I suggested it to her, and as expected, she said "no," reminding me I had a perfectly good doctor, known as one of the best in town. Yes, it may sound like my wife was acting like a mother of an adolescent, which is exactly how it was after the hospitalization... at least for a while.

Months passed, and Dr. Ryce periodically reached out. One such call fortuitously arrived while on our family's spring break vacation to Sarasota, Florida. Intending to let him know it would take a miracle to have me attend his intensive, I called him back. Though he is from Missouri, on that day, quite surprisingly, he and his wife, Jeanie, were just a few miles down the road from me. A friend had lent them their condo for the same week!!! I quickly agreed to meet for breakfast. Even Liz was amazed at this apparently divine hand at play. After an enlightening meeting and experiencing his generosity (a gift of a dozen DVDs with his workshop material) Liz and I agreed I would attend the intensive.

The tools he taught were amazing and effective. He had been training people with them for over forty years, and I especially liked their ancient roots with modern applicability. His presentation allowed my scientific mind—trained as an engineer—to be satisfied while comforting my spirit with love, peace, and true forgiveness. It all mapped well with my Catholic heritage.

I returned home from the intensive with confidence and a renewed spirit. However, my enthusiasm was met with fear and uncertainty. Liz was skeptical and did not care for Dr. Ryce or anyone encouraging my fantasy of getting well. She did not believe it. My Psychiatrist did not believe it. I felt on my own. Over the next few years, I would be on and off medication and in the hospital two more times.

The third time in the hospital, I was terrified I would actually hurt someone. My mind had been presenting thoughts of killing, which was terrifying. As I laid in the hospital bed one night, I saw a vision of dozens of future alternatives play out. All of them ended with me and others dying at my hand. Remember Hercules and my fear? I had to stop it. Without another alternative at that moment, I attempted to end my life. I'll spare you the details, obviously and thankfully, I lived. I soon realized how much I wanted to live and began to research possible solutions, such as the tools referenced in this book. Amongst other things, they taught me how to face fear and stop the cycling thoughts that haunted my mind.

I excitedly went to my doctor with a nutritional product that helped with bipolar symptoms. He answered that he could not recommend it unless there were significant case studies with double-blind testing. Infuriated, I threw the pills in his trash and told him I needed to find a new doctor. Liz began crying, followed me to the hall, and begged me to change my mind.

I responded, "I want to find people who believe that I can get well, not stay with someone who thinks I have a hardware issue requiring him and his medications to keep my brain 'glued' together."

Soon I found an integrative psychiatrist who turned out to be amazing. On the same day, Liz found an M.D. equally amazing. I saw both of them. Albert Mensah, M.D., focused on getting nutrients to the brain. The psychiatrist, Don Raden, focused on healing the gut so that the physical system could function more optimally. Both supported my body being restored to functioning well. Annual lab tests proved my body was strengthening, in balance, and healthy overall.

Additionally, as I practiced the tools from Dr. Ryce and another modality from Dr. Cotton called Higher Brain Living, I began to notice that my inner teacher was helping me way more than I had previously known. I went from being divided and at war with myself to united and in peace. My judgments fell away rapidly, and negative and destructive patterns changed. My body, mind, spirit, and emotions began operating and functioning harmoniously. It was quite spectacular. It was the human version of the caterpillar surrendering its past in exchange for an unknown something. I never got my wings, but I am now living a very fulfilling life.

As I became well, a desire grew to share what I was profoundly affected by, tools that anyone could use for optimal living. I formed a small group of participants to learn the tools in a corporate context. Years of study and practice and feedback resulted in the Optimal Being® program by the fall of 2016. It was a big success!!! One attendee claimed he was more productive in those weeks than he could ever recall. Another doubled her billing rates, got her biggest speaking gig ever, and soon was offered and accepted her dream job. Participants had powerful stories personally and professionally.

The work was always meant for more than just business leaders, though, and we expanded our focus in the spring of 2017 to launch a 501c3 mental health resource hub known as Journey's Dream. We kicked off its inaugural "Soldiers of Hope" event at Soldier Field, home of the Chicago Bears football team. Our inspiration was my recovery and the hope that all people could find their path to health again. My co-founders wanted the same for others after the loss of Journey Montague-Bauer, their son and brother.

Journey ended his life of 25 years in March 2013. He was diagnosed as schizophrenic and on five medications when he walked off a six-story parking garage. He thought if he could fly, yes fly, he could "do the impossible" and heal. His family wanted to honor Journey and the millions who attempt to end their suffering through death by opening pathways for fully living. Journey's dream was to heal fully, and Journey's Dream is serving that mission.

Back to leadership, as we sit in 2020, hundreds of participants have benefited from learning and living the Optimal Being® program's principles. Graduates are equipped to live fearlessly as their true selves: no masks, no pretense. Leading effectively is magnificently enhanced by Awakening the Optimal Leader. This begins by living as an Optimal Being.

End of Non-Fiction and

Begin Visionary Fiction in the year 2037....

CHAPTER ONE

LEAVING THE NEST

It was late Friday afternoon, a bright, sunny, shining day. Rookha Group had just broken its own record for the fifth time, and everyone was excited. In the office, we celebrated with champagne and appetizers. Confetti and balloons covered the floor. The sun came in through the floor-to-ceiling windows and beat down on everyone as the air conditioner cooled us off. But, as it got to be close to 6:00 p.m., I realized it was really time to get home. As I left, it was just another great day at the office to most people. But to me, the joy in my heart was on full overflow—not that I had always felt that way—but today I did. My wife, Liz, and our five children were awaiting a big dinner, and there would be a celebration at home as well. Today was Liz's birthday.

Liz was turning sixty, and I wanted to celebrate in a big way. I made reservations at The Waxed Moon, a posh, new fifties-themed restaurant that was the hottest place in town. As a painter, I knew Liz would revel in all the vintage posters of cars and pinups that bedazzled the walls. Liz and I arrived at the restaurant, and I scanned the dining room and immediately spotted the dark caramel-colored head of our second-born son, Charlie. Beside him was his college-sweetheart-now-wife, Sarah, and their ten-year-old daughter, August, already seated and waiting for us in the big Cadillac-themed booth. Our other four children and their families trickled in after us. We ordered, and when the food came, I prayed over our joyous occasion that peace would come upon this table, and continue to allow for love and laughter to be shared.

It was nearly time for The Waxed Moon to close, and our party was winding way, way down. Most of our family had taken the young grandchildren home, and the only ones to stick around were Charlie and his wife and daughter. Charlie and I had grown to have a profound love and respect for each other over the years working together at Rookha Group. And, I could tell he had something he wanted to bring up, but was looking really uncomfortable about it. He kept looking into his glass of wine, as if it was some kind of movie screen, as he always did when figuring out how to speak about something that embarrassed him. Just then, Sarah came over and laid a hand on Charlie's shoulder.

Bending to his ear, her red curls brushing his cheek, she said, "Your mom is getting tired. I thought I'd just take her home and leave you two to sit a while longer. Mm?"

Charlie nodded and patted her hand. Setting down his glass with deliberation, he said, "Let's move to the bar, Dad."

That brought me to a smile. He knew I loved hanging out with family as much as possible. Charlie and I grabbed seats at the bar, and I signaled the bartender to order our beers when I noticed Charlie was twiddling with something. It was a pen, and I chuckled to myself—he always had something in his hands. I remembered when he was growing up, he'd sit quietly with his stuffed puppy blanket, rubbing its soft ear. It was a way for him to connect lovingly with that inner being, focused on something, yet distant. Now, he was twiddling with the pen, doodling a little bit on the bar napkin and almost *tuning in* to his thoughts and words. I could tell that it was not an easy conversation and attempted to break the ice, knowing that Charlie was just going to go at his own pace.

I leaned my arms on the bar and said, "Whenever you'd like to share what's on your mind, I'm all ears."

"Well, here's the thing, Dad," Charlie began. "I have just found that I have a desire to go and do something on my own. I know we've been working together a while, I've been able to make a lot of contributions, and we've done some great things." He sighed to his freshly poured beer. "I'd like to use the skills I've been developing and apply them in a different field that is just a little more —" he groaned a little.

"It's all right, son. Go ahead."

"You see, I've always loved doing things that create and allow for people to be entertained and have fun. When people are coming from states of denial and dissociation, states of discomfort and lack of confidence, and really move into living as their optimal beings, I feel fulfilled. I think I've done what I came here to do, and that is so much fun."

I glanced over at Charlie to see if he was smiling, his hazel eyes beaming, and he looked back at me.

"We're doing things that are impacting people, but I'd like to see people using the tools and the games and tools that I'm building and take it in another direction. You see, Dad, there is this company. I've known some of these guys for a while, and they're at a point where we were way back when. I think I am being called to that. I'm drawn to be able to create from the ground up. They are on the verge of getting funding, and when they do, I'd like to go help them."

Hearing this reminded me of when I began Rookha Group, but I had to address the basic concerns. "When you say 'on the verge', how close are they?"

"You know how funding is. It could be — I don't know — it could be as soon as next Friday because they are closing a potentially big round, and if that goes through, they think that will lead to another round within about four to five years that will really take them to the next level. The round that's in the works now would be plenty to bring me on and build the kinds of projects that, well . . . "

I could tell he was struggling again, drawing in the sweat of his beer glass.

"You don't know this, but we've been kind of napkin-developing it over the course of the last seven to eight months. Now it looks like it might be a reality. At first, they just asked if I . . . I didn't plan on leaving, Dad."

"That's okay, tell me more."

Charlie cleared his throat, a smile hiding at the corner of his mouth, "At first, they knew I was pretty good at what I was doing, and so they asked if I would help. I just wanted to shoot the shit and have some fun with friends. Well, then it started to get exciting. I saw that as a company it would be a lot of fun, and I let them know, 'Hey, if you ever got funding, I'd like to talk.' That's where I'm at."

I put my beer glass down with a small thud. "All right, well, I suppose this is the part where I give you my fatherly advice."

"Heh, and it *is* world class, Dad," Charlie mused with a wink.

But, there were some serious issues to address. "First things first, the very thing that I believe created my challenges in 2011 — "

"You mean when you were crazy?" Charlie piped in.

"Yeah, yeah," I said, waving that off. "If I had trusted the feelings that had been coming up when they first began . . . " I paused. "It was actually in 2006 that I initially had the inclination to sell my first company. I stressed for some time and failed to trust. I experienced a knowing that I belonged somewhere else and this is where I belonged. Despite financial success in 2007 and 2008, that urge to leave returned with strength in 2009. A few of us, including my then-business partner, Joel, did an exercise to envision our futures. Mine was to sell my interest in the company and move on. The vision was very specific."

I took a gulp of my cold stout brew. "Finally, in 2010, it happened, nearly exactly as I had envisioned it. I might have been a bit too focused on me and not on *all* at that time, but it went the way it went. I had eventually judged that I wasn't in the right job—not in a place where I was at my best. I was letting a lot of people down by working like that."

Charlie nodded. Maybe that was something like what he was feeling?

"You bringing this up," I said, "reminds me that I'm a different guy, now. I had to release the idea that the work I had done in my first company was not the best that I could do. Of course, with the tools I have today, the work I did there would have gone differently. But that was me then, and we need to be who we are in the time that we're in." I put my hand on his broad shoulder. "This is the time you're in. You're feeling this call, and I have always encouraged you to trust yourself. I love that you're coming to me."

"You do?" Charlie looked surprised. "I thought you'd be disappointed."

"On the contrary, I feel so much joy! To have someone, whether it's you, my son, or anyone—but especially you, or any of my children—to have you come and allow yourself to be the very best person first and then to bring into the world your gifts and apply them where you're feeling the greatest amount of joy—my goodness—I want that for all my children and all our grandchildren. That is what your mom and I have wanted for you. Whatever we can do to support you in the transformation to move into that position and be the best you, we're on it."

Charlie grinned, but sat back and he thought a moment. Then he straightened and said, "Listen, there is something."

CHAPTER TWO

COMPETITION

About a year earlier than this news from Charlie, Breaha, one of Rookha Group's founding members, wanted to stretch herself by working for another company. She was so intuitive, and we trusted her implicitly. She began working for Joanne, the CEO of Rock Bottom Hell, an organization attempting to do what Rookha Group does. Well, that's not the actual name of her company; it's just what Breaha used to call it.

While I was conducting a board meeting after Breaha left, I mentioned a little bit about this competitor of ours. The board wanted to hear more, so I began to tell them about Joanne. Breaha had just begun working as the marketing executive in Joanne's company, with the understanding that it was a path toward running the place. It didn't take long for Breaha to have concerns about her CEO, and she consulted me for support.

Apparently, Joanne had been to some of our seminars and had chosen to take the material and begin this competing organization. But her vision was a little different than that of Rookha Group. Her vision was to make as much as she could while on this planet and use our ideas as a way to do it. The program she developed sounded similar, and the delivery may have even been effective, but the intention was impure.

***

Six months into Breaha working for Joanne, they were in a board meeting, and it went sideways fast.

"You have got to be kidding me!" Joanne shouted at the room. "Are you all imbeciles? Can you please?" She slammed a stack of papers onto the meeting table. "Can someone *please* let me know who approved this marketing message? Who sent this out?"

Breaha looked at all the faces around the table. They were blank—stunned—yet not surprised. Everyone seemed to be sitting at the edge of apathy. Half the room had checked out, looking at their phones as Joanne flipped through the papers, fuming. Breaha sat there wondering if she still wanted to work there. Joanne's ways had become tiresome.

Joanne, as she got closer and closer to the death

spiral that was going to kill possibly her and certainly her business, would get frustrated, furious, and angrier by the day. For Breaha, this long, long meeting had just gotten a lot longer. Joanne was beginning her customary task of berating each individual around the table.

"We look like amateurs with this. I thought I was absolutely clear in my instructions for the pitch! No one leaves until this is fixed!"

Breaha felt that Joanne didn't have compassion for her team. Joanne viewed her team members as objects — widgets that were replaceable — and she did replace them. Four people on Breaha's team were fired and replaced in the eleven months she'd been the marketing executive. Not that any of them were bad at their jobs. Joanne would fire somebody if she thought she, herself, looked bad and could blame them. There were other justifications, but ultimately, Joanne was an insecure leader. And Joanne didn't mind crossing the line to usurp Breaha's responsibilities in her own department. Breaha's only feeling of solidarity in this place was that, for some reason, Joanne liked her.

Yet here they were, almost bankrupt in every sense of the word. Breaha knew they had about one payroll left. After that, the company would be out of cash. The marketing message was critical and her team had busted their butts to make it everything Joanne had asked for — to make her the dominating competitor that she wanted to be.

Breaha knew that Joanne thought she could beat Mark at his own game — that Joanne knew Rookha Group's strategy. Joanne had not only studied the company, but was constantly trying to ferret out his strategy through people who had been in his presence, such as Breaha. Joanne thought she knew how to beat him. For Breaha, it felt compromising personally and professionally.

In this latest marketing message, Joanne was attempting to use Mark's own language against him to undermine him. Breaha was beginning to see that in some sad way, Joanne did things like this in order to support her own warped sense of well-being. Yet, the harder she tried, it seemed like the more delusional and mistaken she was about her own situation.

Just before the meeting with the marketing team, Joanne had met with the CFO, Miles. Breaha's office was adjacent to Joanne's, and sometimes she could overhear when Joanne got loud. In meeting with the CFO, Joanne shared the news about how much cash they had left. She then pressed Miles to lie to his team.

"We can't let the team know about this," Joanne said, a little softer, but still audible through the thin walls. "If this ever got out, we'd be finished. People would leave. We can't have that. We need everybody here."

"But Joanne, how are you going to keep people here by continuing to yell and demean them?" the CFO fired back.

"Get out of my office!" Joanne finally said, sounding so shrill that Breaha could imagine her bronzed skin glowing red hot.

Feeling that Miles might need someone to talk to, Breaha went out to find him. She saw Miles' dark brown head bowed over the refreshment counter in the break room. "Hey Miles, um . . . I couldn't help but overhear some of that. You okay?"

Miles just shook his head, "I'll tell ya, Breaha, I'm just dazed and confused. I'm thinking I should just blow the cover off the lid and let everybody know the truth, but then I'm wondering if that is my responsibility. And then there's the matter of honoring my employment contract on confidentiality."

Miles looked up at Breaha and she could see a faint reddening had creeped up above his collar.

"How can I go on not saying a word? I'm only to speak with her about the finances. She'll present to the team what she wants." He leaned in to speak lowly, "All roads lead through Joanne. If she doesn't approve it, it doesn't get done. Now we're faced with a complete disaster."

CHAPTER THREE

BRINGING OUT THE BEST

"Gather around. Everybody, grab a seat," I said as I entered the conference room, while some grabbed coffee and scones. There were sixteen chairs around a long oval table made of handpicked mahogany. Beautiful tall rectangular windows looked out upon lots of greenery. The sky had begun a gorgeous orange sunset. I called the meeting to order, and all the top lieutenants in the organization were there.

"Charlie has something that he'd like to share with everybody. I am going to give him the opportunity to do so, and then we will get into business. Charlie, you've got the floor."

I sat at the back curve of the table, and Charlie came to the front, all eyes on him. A PowerPoint presentation was behind him, and it was a vision for the organization. Charlie presented a way for product development to move in a rapid way with all of the same brilliance that had been developed over the years. But Charlie had also grown rapidly; he was no longer the young man being guided by an older mentor, but was in the driver's seat. Charlie had free rein over this project and gave one of his best presentations. He lit up the room. There was so much energy about what Charlie was presenting.

At the end, Charlie took a sip of coffee and said, "The only challenge that we have here is that I'm going to be moving on."

There was a gasp, and it felt like the room deflated like an old party balloon.

The sales manager shook her head. "But Charlie, the vision you just shared, what about the future of product development?"

Charlie's mentor, though semi-retired, was Rex.

"What would it take to keep you here? You know you could have my department," Rex said. "I don't have a vision like that. I'd work for someone with a vision like that."

"You would?" Charlie said.

Rex nodded his head. "Oh yeah."

Then I piped in, "Don't sell yourself short. You're an amazing leader, Charlie. In fact, everyone around this table . . . " and I began to go person by person and shout out the great things that each person had done to contribute to the success of the organization, until the whole place was beaming again.

"But you know what?" I said. "There is something that your boss said that I think is right. What he is acknowledging is that you're ready for this, Charlie. Your career path is yours to lead if you choose. I think that we would all support giving you anything you needed," I said, looking around the table at all the nodding heads. "You need to do what's best for you, go where your heart is. Would you mind sharing with us what it is you really want to do? What is your desire?"

At the front of the room, Charlie put down his cup of coffee and shared his heart's desire. Now, it wasn't the first time that something like this had happened in Rookha Group. In fact, it was a pretty commonplace thing. If someone had something to share—felt moved—they were free to bring an issue or an opportunity in front of the group. We didn't take for granted that most people don't experience being in a group like this anywhere in their life—at work, at home, even sometimes in their communities— but we had it here. Charlie had brought his talents to Rookha Group, but now he had an opportunity, not only for our organization, but also for himself.

He almost seemed to float as he spoke. He knew his vision was great. But he also felt conflicted.

He shared the story he had shared with me after his mother's birthday celebration. He placed his hands firmly on the big, mahogany table and said, "Okay, everybody. I knew when I was a little kid who I was. I knew my strengths, but I have often been scared to act upon them. I've had this environment that has been so nurturing and loving here, and now it feels like it's time for me to go and put out into the world everything I've learned."

He cleared his throat. "What we have here is great, and we have had so much impact on so many organizations. But for me, I see an opportunity to take the programs we've created here further through gaming. Some of it isn't a good fit here; I am ready to lead and create something new.

"I have a dream to go out and build organizational development tools that are fun. It's kind of the next level of what we are doing here. Imagine transformation by entertainment—and not entertainment as in sit in front of a TV, or go to a movie, or play something on a device; I'm talking about the true nature of entertainment, the true love that each person has within their heart—and bringing that fully into their environment, no matter what they are doing: raising their children, going to school, going to work. Imagine if every one of those situations could be done with a degree of heightened sensitivity to the joys of the self and others.

Now imagine it being trained and ingrained at an early age. If we are successful, companies won't need Rookha Group. The leadership teams and organizations will come equipped with all the tools needed for optimal success through their primary and secondary education. And get this: our main product development team is aged ten through twenty-four years old. We are learning from the younger generations and bringing their needs to the forefront instead of waiting to unwind dramas and traumas later."

Charlie stood up straight and broad-shouldered. "Working on these ideas with some friends of mine is really where I got pulled in, and they've gotten another round of funding. I said no the first time, but now, I feel it's time for me to say yes. I really appreciate my dad giving me the opportunity to present to you today. I appreciate the accolades for the vision, but I am not the only one who can carry out this vision. What I can do is steward it. So, what I'd like to do is offer Rookha Group my time for about four to five hours a month, to maintain the stewardship of the vision. I'll go off and build the organization that I was just sharing with you, but I will still be accessible. And then, if you decide that it's no longer applicable or helpful, I'll stop. How does that sound?"

There was a resounding *yes* around the table.

"Ah, Charlie, that would be great," said Rex. "But who is going to fill your shoes?"

"Well, I have an idea. There are a couple of folks on my team." He named Sean and Hannah, who were pretty young, but he thought together, with him making sure the vision was upheld, they could be successful and groomed to take over.

"Just like each one of you has been developed, these two will develop, too. They are so ripe for this role, and they share the vision. In fact, I'd like to bring them in so that they can share just how clear the vision is."

Even I didn't know that this was going to be part of the presentation. But, Charlie had put so much thought into this transition, there was another round of yesses from the table.

Sean and Hannah came in, only in their late twenties— fresh out of school, master's degrees—I knew them to be very talented. They gave the same presentation pretty much as Charlie had, not word for word, but the spirit of it was conveyed. I was blown away.

Looking around the table, I knew the team saw it, too.

Rex sat forward and said, "Look, with Charlie gone from the organization full time but still stewarding, we can deliver on this."

Sean and Hannah discussed the resources that would be needed and the course and a plan with a schedule. When the whole room applauded, it was no surprise to me or Charlie, but Sean and Hannah were visibly taken aback. Hannah ran her fingers through her long, black hair, nervously looking at Sean. Sean's dark brown eyes darted from behind his steel-rimmed glasses to Hannah, then around the table and back to Hannah again. The applause went on for several seconds, and then slowly everyone around the table began to stand and applaud.

Rex smiled and said, "You're our team."

CHAPTER FOUR

CONFRONTATION

"You must be joking." Breaha, the head of marketing, approached Joanne in her office. "You berated my entire team in front of me. We are friends."

They *had* become friends. Breaha stood there frustrated, watching Joanne, backpedaling, unsure whether to fight and destroy this young woman or come at her with kid gloves to gently manipulate her into staying. Joanne started to justify her actions to convince Breaha that what she had shared in the meeting was important. She talked about how essential it was for some in that room to see her strength. If Joanne didn't show strength, she was afraid that one of the others there might see weakness and then come after her.

Joanne might have pulled that crap on her earlier in her career, but Breaha was much wiser than Joanne had given credit to, and called her on her bullshit.

"That's just not true." Breaha looked Joanne square in the eye. "You're scared, and you're hiding something. And I know it."

"How can you say that to me?" Joanne said.

Breaha took a deep breath, "Because, despite the devious things that we have been doing in our company, I'm aware of how these tools we market actually work. I'm aware of the source from which they come. You didn't create them."

"Yes, I did," Joanne said.

"No, Joanne, these life strategies have been around for a long time. These transformational skills came down through the ages, from a variety of frameworks, including ancient wisdom that informed our religions. And I know them because I have been practicing and benefiting. from them for years. So, I can see your bullshit when it shows up. One of the fruits of the spirit is to see truth. You're not being truthful. You're lying, and I'm out of here if we don't square this away now."

Joanne was floored. Not only was she about to go bankrupt, but Breaha, one of her favorite employees, was calling her on the carpet and threatening to leave, which would destroy any hopes of recovery. Joanne took a step back, her face reddening, breath quickening. "Well Breaha, little do you know, not only is my business life in turmoil, but I also have personal challenges going on too. I'm not on good terms with my mother. I barely see my husband and kids. Everything seems to be just falling apart. And I feel like everyone is out to get me," she said, with tears welling up under her dark blue eyes.

But Breaha was wise to that. "Listen. You want to play the victim. You would love it if I would come and save you. Then you'd feel good and manipulate me to stay. But I'm not playing the game. Stop it."

Joanne slumped down in her chair, deflated. "This is all true, though. My life's a wreck," she said.

"Your life might be a wreck, just don't blame other people. Don't make a sad story out of something that you had a hand in creating. I'm here for one reason. I believe this work is good. But there has to be another way to get this work out, or *I am* out of here."

Joanne crumpled in her chair and looked down blankly at her tailored beige suit. She looked like a tired animal stuck in the mud.

CHAPTER FIVE

CELEBRATING SUCCESS

Seven months went by after Charlie left Rookha Group to start a new company, and Sean and Hannah were a huge hit. Now, they were pretty young, and they made mistakes. Some of it was just that they didn't anticipate a few of the roadblocks that were going to come their way, but in large part, they knew the core principles of the organization and they lived them. Their hires were exceptional, and the team wholly supported each hire they needed. Their timelines, though, weren't exactly a hit. They were within about 20 percent of time and budget targets, which was acceptable for where the organization was.

The first product that launched was a huge flop, and it was a big disappointment to Sean and Hannah. The rest of the team rallied, understanding what a flop was—an opportunity to see what had been produced and grow from it, learn from it. It wasn't that we had gone in the wrong direction or in the right direction. We had made some choices, and put out a product, and it wasn't received as well anticipated. One of the things I had Sean and Hannah do was go visit customers with Charlie. Charlie was working more than the time he had committed, but went out and supported Sean and Hannah in meeting with business leaders to find out what they liked and didn't like.

What Sean and Hannah discovered was about 90 percent of the application was working well. The other 10 percent was minor in terms of the corrections needed, but major in terms of the experience of program participants. The trouble spots were consistent. They went back to the drawing board, made the modifications to the program they had flopped with, and launched again.

The next version was well received, but not at the level Sean and Hannah had hoped. Still, it was good. They started to turn positive cash flow eight months after that. Within a year from the original presentation Charlie had given, Sean and Hannah went from a presentation in a board room to a solution that was being well received. Even though the marketplace was heralding it as a success, Sean and Hannah knew they could make it even better.

One of the things we determined early on in forming Rookha Group was to act as if we had no competition. We were determined to look at the market, find the need, and fill the need. We would deliver the very best product and service we could. We would celebrate that our success would be their success. If the customers were getting the value, then we were succeeding.

As an organization, we looked at what we'd done and asked: *How would we even go beyond that? What would customers want next?*

A year and a half after Charlie's original presentation, the program was being so well received that Sean and Hannah started to believe they had a hit. It still had a few other evolutions before they'd be fully happy with it. But a hit's a hit. Even though the customers didn't know what was coming, they liked what they had. So, Sean and Hannah celebrated and brought the team together and began to explore expansion.

Sean and Hannah also began decommissioning the things that no longer served the market. As CEO, I realized the organization was ripe for success and there was still opportunity, but I was a little nervous when Sean and Hannah came into my office with another new idea. They suggested creative destruction to decommission some of their products and focus on globalization of the best of their portfolio of solutions.

Sean and Hannah had an idea that if they could get into India, which had been blooming, and if they could move from India to China, that we would soon expand our reach around the globe. China had become a powerhouse economically, and it was time to move in that direction and open up those markets. It was time to start translating our program into more languages. It was time to accelerate, but that was going to take capital.

I had been in this situation before, allocating a big chunk of capital serving a larger market. And the value of taking this risk was the positive impact on the organizations and lives we serve. If Sean and Hannah could get the program into these countries over the next three to five years, we would be on track to reach all the people in our target market within a decade. I heard them out, and quickly suggested they meet with the rest of the team to approve the funds. It was an opportunity that I thought was right on target.

Using all the traditional means of communication available, Sean and Hannah began expansion. They became known in the marketplace for not selling; they became known for *Being*. People enjoyed being around them, and conferences were different at the Rookha Group booths. It was a pleasure to be in a space where people could gather, share stories, and hear the different wisdom of the people who would come by because it always attracted the highest and the best.

Rookha Group never really sells in the traditional sense, People seem to be called to it when they are ready. Our intention is to create products that resonate with people's desire to live optimally. When well-being is a priority our offerings become interesting.

Though many have been positively affected, it was a memorable moment when the United States President acknowledged our having impacted social reform at a time when it was most needed. Our role was working with leaders who were implementing social reform policy, supporting the best of who they were to show up in the spirit of collaboration.

Just as a human being might go through Maslow's hierarchy of needs and get to self-actualization, Sean and Hannah were demonstrating how an organization, public or private, can "self-actualize" by focusing on employee well-being

When I look at social statistics from all over the world, and compare it to Rookha Group's customers, I see they have healthy relationships inside and outside their organizations. They are actively engaged. This reflects in profitability and job satisfaction. Employees and teams consistently support themselves and the people around them in lifting their skills—not just their skills in the workplace, but their skills at being optimal leaders and optimal human beings. These are organizations that truly care about life.

CHAPTER SIX

COLLISIONS

Joanne was able to convince Breaha, her young marketing executive, to stick around for another six months. By the sixth month, the situation wasn't a whole lot better, so Joanne was becoming more and more open to solutions. She opened up to listening, and started to question her own BS, wondering what she told herself. Was it true, or was she being delusional, as it had been said about her?

A Thursday evening rolled around with a conference beginning. Joanne got her badge and walked to the main ballroom. There was to be a keynote speaker and then dinner, before everyone would turn in for the night. After the keynote, she sat down at a table next a familiar looking gentleman. He was finely dressed with salt-and-pepper hair, who looked inviting, so she thought he'd be a good person to have a dinner conversation with. She turned and started to ask a little bit about who he was. He began, "My name is Mark."

She said, "Oh, hi, Mark. I'm Joanne." And she brought up her open hand.

***

When I first met Joanne, I did not realize it was Breaha's Joanne, and she didn't recognize me. So, what ensued naturally was just an unfolding of being present, and looking for the very best in her as I had come to do in everyone. I inquired about her and what she had looked to find at the conference. Joanne began to share about her company's programs. Though she was trying to sell me, I was excited to recognize a similar approach as our Rookha Group.

"We're doing something very similar. Perhaps we could collaborate?" But then I saw a shift in her expression.

Joanne instantly had her guard up and stopped talking about herself. She started to ask probing questions. I had seen this strategy before. She was a competitor, trying to fight and get an edge. I began to wonder if she was the CEO that Breaha had been working for.

I leaned a little closer and said, "I will share with you a strategy that I learned about four years ago."

"Oh?" she said, her arms folding in front of her.

I nodded. "The world's changing. There are no more competitors. If you want to get me to tell you about my trade secrets so that you can manipulate that and then go beat Mark and his big company in the market, that's just fine. You can have all the answers you want. Why don't we grab a drink? You can ask whatever you want, and I'll share what you'd like."

"What?" she said, blinking. "What, really?"

"Of course."

Joanne shifted in her seat uneasily. She looked around the conference room, "You are kidding, right? Is there a hidden camera here somewhere?"

"No," I said, a little amused.

She rubbed her tanned jaw thoughtfully. "Okay, let's grab a drink after."

"Terrific!"

***

After dinner, Joanne and I found a spot near the pool outside. It was a beautiful moonlit night. Lots of people were conducting business meetings in this area. We found a little table and a couple chairs, and cocktails were quickly served to us. It only took about fifteen minutes for me to share Rookha Group's entire strategy. Joanne sat feverishly, reaching into her bag and thumbing her notepad now and then. I figured she wanted to write notes, but felt embarrassed to take out a pen and paper and write. For a long time, she didn't take her eyes off my face, so she was doing her best to just remember everything.

Then, at the end, I said, "If you ever want to come down and check out our operation, we'd be happy to have ya."

"What? Are you kidding me? That's the weirdest thing I've ever heard!"

I could tell by our interactions where she was.; frightened about her business...nervous. I acknowledged it and brought up an opportunity to. that could be constructive for her.

For a few moments, Joanne just sat glancing at me sideways—like she couldn't quite figure out my agenda. I was kind, open, and truly willing to work with her, but deliberately didn't ask anything specific about her company. I knew a little, but not much, not tlhat she had nearly identical products and services, and I didn't know that her company was on the verge of bankruptcy. Joanne did her best to play her cards close to the vest.

When we completed the evening, I said, "You know, I want to share one last thing with you. If you believe that your programs are better, and they are being executed more effectively than the ones we are selling, I would love to license your programs and your delivery teams. We want to give our customers the very best quality products and services in the market, period."

"How would that work?" she asked, opening up a little.

"My group loves to innovate. They love it when someone comes up with something even better than what we have today. We try to do this internally, but if it happens externally, we will just as quickly look for opportunities to collaborate with someone or resell someone's product so consistently deliver the optimal value. If yours is the optimal value, let's forge a relationship so everyone benefits."

Joanne leaned forward, but spilled her drink. She stood, and tried to wipe herself off and pull herself somewhat together. She said, "Look, Mark, everything we have talked about tonight is the opposite of everything I learned in business school. I can't even believe I am being this open with you, but I think you're quite nuts."

"Oh, yeah, probably," I said with a serious tone.

"What do you mean?" she said.

"I was certified *nuts,* I suppose, when I was younger."

"What?" she said.

"Anyone who is divided internally with an untrained personal code is a bit *nuts,* wouldn't you say?"

"How so?" she asked.

"When people are divided, what is happening is they are trying to serve multiple masters. Some people are serving twenty to thirty masters within the same body. I chose to serve one." I held up one finger.

"What do you mean?" she said, sitting back down.

"It's the source of all. It's the very Creator, the essence of being, that brought forth life. That is where I rest my energies. Anything outside of that, forget it. That is why, when you are trying to pick my brain and get a competitive advantage, I am just giving it to you." I chuckled, "And you are freaking out."

"Wait, how did you know that?" She caught herself. "You know, maybe we should just wrap up. I've had a few too many."

"It's okay if you want to leave, but if there is an opportunity for us to collaborate, then let's talk. I don't know what the state of your business is, but here are our numbers." And I brought out my notepad and pen and wrote down our revenue, plus gross and net margin.

"Wow, you guys are making a lot of money," Joanne said, leaning over the paper.

"Well, it's easy when you are working with amazing people developing and delivering exceptional offerings." I was attempting to be honest and could see her growing discomfort.

"Yeah, but what about all your overhead and everything? What about productivity?"

"Our teams are highly efficient," I said.

"You can't have that high efficiency of a team. These numbers are ludicrous."

"We do," I said, sitting back and pushing the paper toward her. "It took several years to get here. Our experience, though, is that another organization can get there in about six to twenty months. But it takes a commitment from the top down."

"In six to twenty months . . . " she shook her head. "How would it happen?"

"Your company would completely transform," I said, leaning in.

"What do you mean?"

"Well, we would look at your desires. We'd see if those desires are in line with the spirit and health of the organization and with the individuals leading it. If there are any discrepancies or divisions, as I was sharing, we would look to bring those divisions closer together so that they, too, get resolved and people are tuned in."

"What does that mean, *tuned in?*" she asked.

"Well, when someone is tuned in, their intuitive guidance system informs their every action. Their thoughts are really clear—pure. There is a lot of trust."

"Wow," she said. "That sounds like some of the things we sell."

"Well, it should because that's where the opportunity exists for all leaders to get to the next level of leadership."

Joanne leaned in thoughtfully. "If we could do that even sooner, I'd like it, but six to twenty months, that's huge. I don't think our programs would do it that quickly."

"Well, they might, but it really requires you to live them."

"Me personally?" she asked.

"Of course."

"Well, I'm doing the best I can," she said, looking away.

"Right," I said, turning my wedding band in the moonlight. "How's it working?"

She looked down at my notepad, "You want to know the truth, Mark?"

"Only."

"We're really struggling. We're fighting. My life's kind of a mess. I haven't been true to the people in my organization, haven't treated them with respect. Frankly, I don't know how long we are actually going to make it. If this organization could change and turn around, if my life could start to change and turn around . . ." a little smile spread to her cheeks, "that would be very interesting to me."

CHAPTER SEVEN

COLLABORATION

I agreed to collaborate with Joanne. After spending a couple days at the conference and speaking candidly with her, I said, "Look, there is probably not a chance that we would work with you unless you actually came and understood what our programs are. Then you, along with your leadership team, must adhere yourself to the program. I'd need to see a commitment on your part."

Joanne was hungry at this point. By the end of the weekend, she wanted to do the programs and maybe even resell them. They were clearly stronger than the programs she had. Joanne was willing to take a chance and bring this into her organization. Her spirit of intent was so pure. She asked if I would put together a proposal. So I did.

That week, I went back to Rookha Group to speak to the team. I let them know all about Joanne and what was going on at her organization. The marketing team took a look at the website, and they said it looked a lot like the kinds of programs they would have done about six or seven years ago.

Hannah had her doubts. "She appears to be in this for herself, Mark. Are you sure that she's open?"

I could understand where Hannah was coming from, but I understood where Joanne was, as well. "She's desperate, which isn't the best place for someone to make a choice, so we will put a proposal together that is more than. I suggest we start by offering Joanne and her leadership team four days of free coaching—come into Rookha Group, and just open the books. Share everything with them."

Sean, too, had his concerns. Adjusting his glasses, he asked, "Mark, are you sure that opening our company like that is a good idea with someone like her?"

"No, but it's worth a shot. It will be our biggest test. Breaha went there for a reason. Perhaps, this is it," I said. "What we will propose is to pair our executive teams—marketing with marketing, and so on. Everyone on their teams will go through our programs, and they will have you as mentoring counterparts."

Hannah shook her head. "Joanne seems so selfish, are you sure you want to build up this woman and her business?"

"Hannah, check in with yourself after releasing judgments of this woman. Tune in to what is optimal for all."

Hannah was a pro at tuning in and listening to her inner guidance system. She suddenly took a breath and smiled. "I get a *yes*," she said with a strange look on her face.

"Me, too," I replied. "Let's trust it."

I continued, "I have a feeling I am going to need to be her individual coach, and I believe she would be about six weeks away from having a number of epiphanies. When she does, she is going to realize how to treat people well, how to enter into agreements effectively, and how to change some of the personal relationships that have been struggling. If she can shake her fear patterns, she'll be brilliant. As that occurs, I think we will be better off working collaboratively together than separately."

***

The next month, we brought Joanne and her leadership team in to show the presentation we had set up. The entire interaction was designed for Joanne and her team to experience their potential future on a new trajectory. The four hours it took to present went by very quickly, and at the end of the day, Joanne's entire leadership team was just floored. They couldn't believe how effectively an organization could run. But, Joanne had kept them in the dark, and some anger and hostility crept into the room. So, we extended the meeting another hour and a half to allow for that anger and hostility to be expressed. We helped Joanne's team process through one of our key metrics: love.

When we brought love into that space where anger and hostility arose, it simply started to dissolve. They had frank conversations, very transparent. Joanne was able to see into the hearts of her people, and for the first time, she had a glimmer of what it was like to see them as human beings instead of pawns in her game. It was her beginning to see the essence of who they are. This encouraged Joanne's team enough to stay with it and to watch as she negotiated the project with me.

After negotiations, I had Joanne join me in my office, and had our legal counsel join us. As the lawyers wrote the paperwork, one of the first things

I made clear was, "Any time that you choose to bow out of this, the whole thing's over. I expect 100 percent commitment from you and your full personal participation. This is about your optimal employee well-being being a priority while your organization becomes the very best it can be. And then what follows is that dollars will start to flow. As money flows, you will reinvest into your programs and revise them so they more accurately reflect the true nature of the teachings.

"The same teachings we're teaching, you're teaching in slightly different ways. But you have a couple of nuances. You had designed your programs in such a way that it's about, well, it's about you. And it can't be. If your company is going to be optimally successful, it first needs to place your customers at the forefront, and then your employees, and you're pretty much last." I leaned into her space. "You come last. In coming last, you become a servant to the organization and allow for the people in it to truly thrive. Your products will be improved, your revenues will go up, your profits will go up, and your employees will shift from being extremely hostile and rather disengaged to engaging fully. As this transition happens, you will probably lose a few of them, but it will be for the right reasons. You are setting your organization up to attract people that are right for this environment."

"What do you mean that I'm going to lose people?" Joanne looked a little anxious.

"It may not happen right away. When an organization goes through a transformation, people don't always see that they are a good fit anymore. They may not align to the changes. This can be excellent for them to find a better fit. Trust me. You have an opportunity to truly light the way for your customers, employees, and you. Your life's about to change, but you must be 100 percent committed."

Joanne looked at me and agreed, "100 percent." She looked down at the paperwork that was being put together. "I can't quite believe that I'm saying that. This is going to take a lot of work, but I know, somehow, that everything I've gone through this afternoon, though challenging, is right for all."

Joanne was lightly tapping her fingers, still staring at the paperwork. I thought she must be feeling a bit nervous, so I said, "Look, you're going to do great. Your company's going to be fine. You need to trust. I know that this is a challenge, and it can be rather frightening. But many people are doing this with you, and you're going to go through this with friends."

"Friends?" she said. "Those people are not my friends."

"Yes, they are. You just haven't accepted them. You've pushed them away. I believe you came into this world with pure intentions. Somewhere along the way, it got twisted. It's time to untwist."

She gave a snort of derision. "How are you going to do that?"

"*You* are going to do it."

Joanne looked at me. "What do you mean?"

"All the tools that we just taught, they will unlock within you a transformation. Within every person is what we call *the optimal being*. It's within you, too. There is also a guidance system for every person to find it, to discover it, and to allow it to come to life, to really remind you of the very essence of you, and. Be. the best individual you can be. No matter who you're around, you stay true to who you are. You become the light in the room. Now, when you have an entire organization going through this, big things happen. Not everyone, like I mentioned, is going to want to stay. They will discover they've been doing things for inauthentic reasons. Yet those who do stay will have chosen consciously to realize their full potential along with you.

"You will lead by example, living in your true nature as your optimal being. You will be three steps ahead of your team for a while as we go at an accelerated pace. This will allow you to be aware of what your team will be taught. You will be a leader, a catalyst, a coach. The true leader exhibits coaching qualities and recognizes the brilliance in each person. As you organizationally move from the place you are now and transition to who you are going to become, there will be opportunities for you to use all the tools and skills that your company is going to provide. You will have an opportunity to practice, and practice is the very essence of what this work is about."

"How long do I have to practice?" she asked.

"Truly, it becomes a life skill. Imagine the first time you dribbled a basketball. It wasn't that easy, but you kept going, and you became more proficient. Pretty soon, you could dribble between your legs, you could go around the back, you could make passes in a way that you couldn't when you started, and you could shoot the ball in new ways. Now, imagine practicing tools supporting you fully living as your optimal being all the time."

"Why *being?*" she asked.

"Being is the loving life essence of every human who has ever lived. The brilliance and amazing transformation that can occur is extraordinary. It can happen for you, but it's not just for you. It's for your family, it's for all the people in your company, and it's eventually going to reach your customers and your partners and everybody who touches your organization."

"Is this what you did?" Joanne asked.

"Absolutely, we eat our own *dog food*," I said with a chuckle.

"Yeah, I suppose you do." She smiled. "How does it taste?"

"It's awesome. It's more like a gourmet meal," I leaned back in the chair and patted my belly. But sitting up more seriously, I said, "It doesn't always feel good though, and there are moments. I tell you what, it doesn't always feel that great making the gourmet meal, right? But it sure is enjoyable to eat it. And when you are finished with our program, you are going to have that. Imagine a six-course meal with all the accoutrements and the biggest celebration. That is going to be you and your organization."

"Who will be there with me?"

"All the people who are supposed to be," I said.

"What does that mean?" she asked.

"The people who are optimal to be in your organization will be there."

"Good enough for me," Joanne said. "I'm in."

She reached for her pen and signed a $400,000 agreement. She didn't have $400,000. It was based on the performance of doing the work. The down payment was her home mortgage. She gave me the deed to her home as collateral. It was all she had. I gave her a commitment to perform, and she was willing to do that.

Once she was about to sign on that line, I said,

"Stop." "What?" Joanne looked at me incredulously.

I shook my head, "I don't want your house." "You

don't?"

"No. I want you to be committed. What would it take to make it so that this is the number one priority for you?"

"I'm already in," she said.

"Well, then that's good enough for me. You can leave that line blank." And she did.

Joanne got up. She wasn't normally a hugger, but she reached around and gave me a big hug. "Thank you so much. This is one of the most memorable moments of my entire life. Thank you, thank you, *thank* you."

PART 2

CHAPTER EIGHT

THE FUMBLE

My company and I gave approximately 30 percent of our time to supporting Joanne and her business for six-months. This was quite an undertaking. It felt purposeful, inspired.

Rookha Group employees tend to live attuned to their optimal being state and positive actions follow. This keeps the entire organization in rhythm. There is such a camaraderie that when anyone ever got interested in something else, there is support to learn that new job, and gain those new skills. There is a willingness to allow people to take risks, not just inside, but also outside the company.

Many of the new developments that have happened around Rookha Group and its community are happening in companies that Rookha Group has no ownership in. Employees came in, learned some of the skills, developed, tuned in, and were inspired. Our leadership team and I told them to *Go for it.*

We provided encouragement and support and even handled administrative challenges so they could get on their feet and not have to worry about the many things that often get in the way of a start-up. We stripped the common activities away so they could focus on new product development, innovation, sales, and delivery. There certainly were benefits financially for Rookha Group, and it supported people in the organization really stepping into their dreams.

So, if ever an organization was ripe to spend 30 percent of their time serving the transformation of another company, it would be Rookha Group. It was a dynamic shift that happened when my team and I came into Joanne's organization and began teaching — began practicing — just as I had proposed, two by two. Heads of marketing working together, heads of sales working together, and so on. It became very clear that there were areas of dysfunction in Joanne's organization and our team would call it out. Shocked and horrified at first, Joanne became more and more comfortable with the crap in her company being thrown in the middle of the room.

The first time that her head of marketing, Breaha, shared one of their most significant secrets of dysfunction, Joanne actually threw up in the bathroom. She was there horrified, crying, throwing things around the bathroom, wondering if she had made a horrible, horrible mistake. But I thought it was funny because I and others had been there and gotten through it. And sure enough, each time, as the weeks passed, Joanne saw the emergence of what she hoped could happen, and realized that by putting the "good" and "bad" out in the open, her team could step into the situation and resolve it. It was like taking all the hidden secrets and putting them out there one by one, sometimes even more than one, cringing a little bit, but softening, as everyone looked around the room. My team and I would be there to celebrate it, and Joanne's team would realize, *Okay, let's try this,* and they would join in.

Over the course of the coming weeks, Joanne and her team began to learn a lot of the tools that our team had fully integrated. Joanne's team became proficient, all of them professional, as they gained expertise. Each one of them in their own field was among the best of the best.

As Joanne's team continued to progress, not only did they gain the skills and expertise in their roles, but they had the tools to support the other folks in their organization. They resolved some of their inner demons—those big challenges that everyone was concerned about.

Joanne would say, "Let's bring that out. Let's get it out there. We can then look at it. We can shine a proverbial light upon it and look and see what it is because maybe there is something really good in there. Maybe there is a brilliant strategy that is years old, and it is no longer helping our organization, even if it did at one time."

One of the biggest strategies Joanne's company had to change was in sales. They were using sales in a way that a 1950s sales team would have used. They had a morning meeting where everyone would come in together, and then they would get their leads and start hunting. It was slow. It was ineffective. It was causing a lot of challenges from a speed-to-market standpoint and getting the revenue to where the organization could really thrive.

They were using the old tactics of manipulation: price manipulation, human manipulation, emotional manipulation. They used these core ingredients to get something from their customers. But, Joanne's company attracted customers who were not the optimal customer for this kind of work. They attracted customers who also felt manipulation was a key part of their world. It wasn't a healthy relationship, and it created dysfunctional spirals.

Jared was our sales leader assigned to work with Amy, the head of sales in Joanne's organization. An African American in his mid-thirties, Jared appreciated the step back from his day-to-day, and he loved seeing people succeed. He allowed Amy to realize for herself that her strategies weren't working. She accomplished this by doing three simple things: First, they did a whiteboard strategy so the dynamics in Amy's department could be illustrated. Second, Jared compared the model of his sales team and of Amy's sales team.

Amy saw the problem right away. "Oh my gosh, it would take a hundred years to get to where you guys are. I can see what you are saying. We are stuck in the fifties!"

She was exaggerating the 100 years, of course, so the first thing Jared said was, "What would be optimal is to bring the whole team in and let them know that they are stuck in the fifties, and it's time to let it go."

Amy began pacing in front of the whiteboard. She was starting to hold her breath and suddenly burst out, "I'm not sure this is really going to work."

Jared had seen this before, and smiled inside as Amy tried to justify her position and resist change.

"Look, I get that we are learning and transforming, but this is going too far. Let's pause this for a bit. I need to speak to Joanne about this."

Jared was excited for the free time and texted his wife to invite her and their two children for lunch. "Let me know if you would like me to come back this afternoon," he said as she left the room.

Amy went immediately to Joanne's office. "Joanne, this program must stop."

Joanne looked at her and said, "What do you mean?"

Joanne had been working with me for many weeks and had already seen the benefits and fruits. She was no longer afraid to change at this point, and had become more embracing of our program. She was concerned that one of her leaders wasn't on board.

"Well, Jared wants me to bring my whole team in and expose how I've been doing my job wrong," Amy said, a little clenched.

"Well, have you?" Joanne said, sitting back, relaxed.

Amy paused and stumbled a little bit. "I guess. You know what, Joanne? I fear every day that I'm messing up at home and at work. Now, I have this dude come in and share a completely new way of operating. I don't know if I can go into that level of fear."

"Why not?" Joanne asked.

Amy sat down across from Joanne. "I'm not sure that I trust myself to do it right. What if we scrap our whole sales strategy that I am effective at? What if I can't make the transition? What if then I'm out of a job? I shouldn't even be saying this to you, I suppose. But, I suppose in our new world of putting it out there, I'm putting it out there."

"Keep going. Tell me what's at the root of this. I'm listening," Joanne uncharacteristically urged.

"This seems silly, but lately I keep remembering, well, the first time I felt as I do now," Amy said, her sandy head bent toward the checkered carpet under Joanne's desk. "I had a report in grade school that I was so excited about, and I wanted to do such a good job on it. But I got stuck. I was so stuck that I sat in my room with a stack of books and a piece of paper and a pen, and I had written the word *Introduction*. But I didn't know where to go from there. I had read through a couple of the books, skimming mostly, unsure of what to read, how to read, and how to put a paper together."

Amy sighed. "My mom came in, saw that I was stuck, and offered to help."

Joanne leaned her arms on her desk, listening intently.

"Of course, I said yes. My mom was a writer. In about four and a half minutes, there was an outline done. I looked at it and said, 'Oh my gosh, thank you, Mom!'"

Amy's face began to contort, "Joanne, I'm still holding onto that memory of not being good at something, of not knowing. When I find something that I'm good at, I hang onto it."

Joanne encouraged her and said, "Look, if you let go of a system that isn't working for this organization, that's the right thing to do because it's the right thing to do. The rest of your insecurities and your apparent lack of knowledge is the BS that you are holding on to. For your own sake, let go of this story you're telling yourself, that you're not good. Because the truth is, you *are* a good person Joanne! What you're saying is you're not good at doing some things, but that's everyone. You've shared with me that you're not good at learning new things, and you get stuck when you don't know. You're afraid to ask, and instead of asking someone to do it for you, what you're really wanting is someone to teach you how."

Amy rubbed a hand over her pale forehead. "Yeah, I suppose that is what I've been looking for. That is what I was looking for then. I guess I did want my mom to do it—honestly—because I was in a hurry. I wanted to go out and be with my friends. But you know what? I probably judged that it would have been—"

Joanne stopped her with a shake of the head, "No, Amy. Let go of the judgment. Release the judgment that you didn't do it well, that you couldn't learn. Let all that go. Let go of the judgment that your mom or you should have done it differently."

Amy nodded her head. "Yeah, I've got to release all that." And then she smiled. "I'm already feeling a thousand pounds lighter. I think in telling you just now, I did loosen my hold on it."

"And now, together," Joanne said, "just as we've been taught, we'll cancel out the old ideas we have around sales—all of them—and open up to change."

"Really?" Amy said with a big smile.

"Yes, let the entire sales structure fall away."

"The whole structure, too?" Amy asked, blue-green eyes wide.

"Yes, but it's not about letting it disappear and not using any of what we've known, it's about letting go of the attachment we have to our old ways. You demonstrated that we have been attached to this, and part of it has been because you are insecure about whether you can make a change. You're more comfortable now, but keep allowing for the discomfort to come up."

Amy sat stock still, and Joanne noticed she had started to hold her breath. "Remember what the team has taught us," Joanne said. And she made a motion to inhale, and Amy began to breathe again.

"All right, all right," Amy said, and took a couple of deep breaths. "I'm in. I cancel all of my ideas about our old sales approach and how brilliant it was — how effective it was — because the truth is: it's not producing the outcomes we want. So, I release the attachment I have of trying to hang onto something that is clearly not functional and needs to be changed. And you know what? If I'm not the right person for you, Joanne, then . . ." She looked back down at the carpet. "I certainly understand if you need to bring somebody else in who can do this job."

But then Amy looked back into Joanne's eyes. "I will do the very best that I can," Amy said. But you have to do what's best for the company."

"That's the spirit," Joanne said. "My confidence in you has risen during this conversation. These healthy conversations, they help us get to a place where we can be more functional as a team. This is the kind of raw, absolute transparency that leaders and their teams need to have." Joanne stood up. "And, I expect you to have these conversations with your team."

"Yeah—yes—you're right," Amy said. "You know what? I am going to bring my team together this afternoon. Would you like to join us?"

"Amy, if you think that my being there is going to support you, then I'm there. I will do whatever role you want. However, if you want me to lead the meeting, I'd rather teach you how to be open in front of your team."

"You'd teach me that?" Amy said. And she started to laugh.

"Yes," Joanne said.

"How is it you're going to teach me vulnerability? You're just learning it yourself."

"Practice. I'm willing," Joanne said. "I'm willing."

"Well, I appreciate your courage, Joanne, and I'm willing, too."

That afternoon, Amy gathered her team. When they were all seated in the conference room, it was not only Amy, but also Joanne, and the representative from Rookha Group, Jared. Amy stood up in front of the team. With all her courageous vulnerability, she started to outline the changes that they wanted to make in sales. With compassion, she recognized the discomfort her team might feel in moving from one approach to another.

She strove to foster inclusiveness by saying, "You are going to participate in crafting this, but we are going to get the best of the best to guide us, to teach us, so that we not only are going to open up and shift from where we are, but shift into a team where we are willing to adjust. If the market changes, we will adapt. We don't know where we will end up at this point, but we will trust in the change. I hardly believe I'm even saying that." She laughed, and the team nervously laughed with her.

This transition was a huge breakthrough for Joanne, Amy, and her team. A few of them came up after and said to Amy that they were freaking out. They essentially presented a case similar to the one she had presented to Joanne. Amy didn't yet have all the tools to navigate them through it as Joanne had with Amy, but Joanne and Jared were there with her. Together, they navigated through effectively.

***

Later that night, when Jared had gotten home, he received a call. It was Amy. She was in tears.

"What is it?" Jared asked.

"I have a confession to make," said Amy.

"Yes?"

"I really like you, and I am so happy that you're a part of what we're doing. But I don't believe that I'm the right fit. I don't know how to change as quickly as the organization needs."

"Aw, that's easy," Jared said.

Amy laughed and said, "Easy for you to say."

"No, it's easy," Jared said.

"How is it that you can sit there and tell me that it's that easy, when with all my years of experience I can't see a way forward?"

"Amy, I can tell you honestly that it's that easy because I've been in your shoes. Rookha Group went through this, Amy. You think that suddenly we were just operating in a highly efficient mode? When I was first hired, we were completely dysfunctional. We had poor communication and many unhealthy arguments. We had silos within our silos. And I believed that was the normal way a business runs.

"Amy, I want to share something with you. Back in the beginning of our organization—Mark doesn't talk about this often—he and the partners actually took a hiatus for six months. They shut the whole company down. They didn't do much of anything except explore what it was they wanted to do. Mark actually told Rex, one of the partners, that he wasn't ready to play at the level they needed to play at, and he was thinking of doing this whole organization on his own. When Mark realized that going solo wasn't what he really wanted, he finally came back and reconnected with Rex. He wanted to see how Rex had changed, too.

"Well, it turned out Rex would go on to say that it was the very best thing to ever happen—he was challenged. Mark told Rex that he thought Rex wasn't meeting people where they needed to be met. He was giving a prescription for people instead of allowing for what needed to come up within them. It was a huge growth opportunity for both of them. Mark had discovered a number of things about himself that, had they not taken that six-month hiatus, maybe Rookha Group would've been completely different. You see, neither one of them had the skills at the time to do it differently.

"Today, when issues of how to proceed come up, they surface immediately and come to the forefront. They are addressed in such a loving way that it allows for transformation to happen seamlessly. Instead of going off and doing a lot of processing, the change often happens in a breath. It's really beautiful. And the same thing happened for the rest of us. In my first months, I thought about leaving so many times. But, I didn't, and I am so happy I stayed. My pattern of leaving when things got tough melted away. There were a lot of ups and downs, yet it was all worth it because life is worth being who we actually are and doing what we love doing.

"Amy, if you love doing what you're doing, trust. *Trust*. If this isn't the organization ultimately that is going to support what you want in your life, then— if Joanne is really learning from Mark, and it seems like she is—Joanne is going to celebrate with you and support you as you move on to your next endeavor."

"Really?" Amy said.

"Yeah, really."

"All right," she said, and cleared her throat. "Thank you so much."

"You're welcome. See you in the morning."

CHAPTER NINE

REVOLT

Amy and Miles, the CFO, started to work more closely together on the new programs. Every day after work, they would practice the new strategies they were working on. Their relationship became romantic, and one night, they were sitting at The Southwest Grill across from some nachos, and an issue arose for Amy. The issue was about a past relationship.

Miles had many past girlfriends, and Amy was experiencing a degree of jealousy. She wanted to know all the details, but each detail that he would reveal, though he was hesitant, would trigger even more anger. These details resonated with old frustrations, hurt, and pain within Amy, and she began to project it all on Miles.

Amy realized that the tools Joanne had introduced were also bringing out this old pain. They were allowing her to step deeper into the pain that she had been trying to hide for years. A hurt—a betrayal— that had been so deep that she never, ever wanted anyone to tap into that wound was now coming up to the surface.

Amy did her best to continue hiding using her favorite drug, anger. When angry, her pain seemed to subside. Unfortunately, Miles was the recipient, even though these emotions were about things that happened long before they had ever met. She saw herself as the victim and was out for blood.

Miles was confused, but recognized her deep desire to know more, so tried to explain all these details even though in his mind it was unnecessary.

"Why do you want to know all this?" Miles finally asked.

Amy's eyes welled up with tears, and she slammed her fist right in the middle of the nachos, and said, "I want to know everything. If I am going to be with you, I want to know every detail. I want to know who I'm with because I want to know if you're going to hur . . . ," and she stopped. She clenched her fists, and he realized she was going to talk about how she had been hurt in the past, a story she had never shared with anybody.

She took a deep breath. "I just want to make sure that you are going to treat me well, that I'm going to be safe with you."

"Safe?" Miles said, dazed. "Amy, I don't understand where this is coming from."

It wasn't even, in fact, anything that had necessarily been done to Amy that started her relationship with betrayal. It was a story she heard about a relationship her mother had had, how her mother was scorned and how much pain she carried through her life. Through little quips and stories her mother shared, Amy picked up on it verbally, energetically, and it was probably even a part of her subconscious. She was carrying her mother's resonance of betrayal so that it was present in every moment, wondering who was going to betray her next.

Amy sought relationships and set up situations that would cause the betrayal to come out. It was so upsetting in her life to be in and out of relationships and in and out of jobs. Amy had worked three years at Joanne's organization and had been very comfortable in the environment where people were yelling at each other, hating each other, and backstabbing, because it was a betrayal environment. She got to play in it. She was one of the most. prolific victims, and perpetrators. Amy had developed a talent for betrayal.

But Amy didn't see it that way; she saw it more like she was a soldier in a very big war. Not that it was even a war she ever needed to fight. It was from something that had happened before she was even born. Yet, here she was, playing it out, in Joanne's organization, at the table with Miles, right in the middle of the nachos.

Miles was stunned. He looked at Amy and said, "Honey, all I want to do is be who it is that I am, and in a relationship, find a peace, and a calm, and a love, something that we can nurture and grow together with. But you know what?"

Amy put her glass loudly down on the table. She grabbed a napkin and started to wipe the nachos off her hand. She started to quiver with fear, anger, and sadness — so much emotion rushing through her. "If Joanne had not brought Rookha Group in, this would never have happened. We wouldn't be having this fight."

"But she did," Miles said. "And it's actually good."

"No, it's not. Don't you see how it's destroying everything? It was so good before," she said as a tear hooked onto some mascara, leaving a black streak down her thin cheek.

Miles said, "No, it wasn't. It was a disaster. Look, we are finally making a profit. Joanne is no longer worried every day about making payroll."

"Ugh, so what? I don't even care about that," Amy said. "All I care about is us."

Miles was taken aback. "Well, if all we cared about is us," he said, "then that is not really going to be best for the company."

"So what? I think this needs to stop," she said, pulling herself together.

"What does?"

"This whole program. We have to get rid of this program."

Miles looked at her, stunned.

Amy leaned over the crushed nachos. "Look, you either pick the program, or you pick me."

The ultimatum hung over the mess of nachos, between Miles and Amy, for several minutes. Miles loved this woman. He saw the good in her, her sweet side and her drive. He wanted so much for her pain to stop. Miles had wanted Amy to fall in love with him; maybe he cared more about that than the company.

He pensively rubbed his palms together in thought. "What are you proposing we do?"

"Well," and Amy began to outline a plan to manipulate and subvert the changes Joanne had brought in; her blue-green eyes lit up—dazzling—just like they used to do when she had a client on the hook. There was a power in this look that had always made Miles feel a little uneasy, yet it captivated him. Amy planned to allow for the organization to start to see the cracks the changes were making, and to then divide people up into factions. Once there were enough people sucked into factions, Miles and Amy could tip the scales so that Joanne would have to let the program go.

Miles took a moment to look at her plan, and it was actually a really good—if evil—plan. He had never believed that he would say this, but he said, "You know, I wouldn't do this for anybody else—I am not sure if I want to even do this at all—but I don't think that . . . ." He coughed, something seemed to be stuck in his throat. "Well, I need to think about it. I would like to go think about it."

"How much time do you need?" she said.

"Let me go to the bathroom. I'll be back."

Miles got up, went to the bathroom, and looked in the mirror. Alone there, he began to speak to himself, "Ugggggh!!!! What is happening here!!???" This is ridiculous. The organization went from broke to profitable. Now, Amy wants to undermine it?" He grumbled, "And I am going to help her? For what?" Miles shook his head, torn, "This is stupid. She obviously is hurting. Maybe if I could help her embrace her hurt, she might get after it, resolve it, and then this whole plan will go away. I could just agree to go along with it and find some way in helping her see she is not functioning well, and she needs to resolve what's in her instead of projecting it on Joanne and the company, on the program, on me.

"My god," he said looking at the mirror, frustrated with himself, with Amy. He slammed his palm on the mirror. "Where'd that woman go that I met? That woman who just lit up my heart? This isn't her. It's like an alter ego or something!" Miles started to wash up, dry his tears. "I'm going to go back and confront her. This is stupid. This is just dumb. I've got enough tools—have been at this long enough. It's been four months," and he walked out the door.

Arriving back at the table, he shared his epiphany with Amy. "Before we carry out this plan, do me a favor."

"I ordered us some ice cream. What's your favor?" she asked, cool and sweet.

"I . . ." and suddenly he froze. He was remembering a childhood memory of wanting to say something really important and not being able to get the words out—the other kids all laughing—that's how he felt as Amy just looked at him like he was an idiot. So, he sank into the booth, disoriented, and said, "Okay, fine, I'm in."

"All right!" Amy grinned ear to ear. "Cheers!"

She lifted a glass, and he slowly lifted a glass, knowing sabotaging Joanne wasn't what he really wanted, but he wasn't ready to confront Amy and end their relationship.

***

After weeks of dealing with doubts and difficulties, Joanne too began to wonder if her collaboration with Mark was truly worthwhile. Although her company was still turning a profit, it had slowed down significantly. Joanne had started to wonder if she was the right fit for this type of program after all.

When Miles came into Joanne's office and said he was quitting, Joanne's challenges hit a new level.

"What?" Joanne said with a start. "You, Miles? You're doing so great! You've transformed the finance team. We're moving in the right direction. The numbers are great, and you're quitting?"

Miles didn't sit down, just stood a few feet from the door. "Joanne, there is so much tension in this company, and you might not realize this, but not everyone wants to go into their shit."

"What do you mean?" asked Joanne.

"I was told by . . ."

"Wait, wait, wait." Joanne got up. "Please, let's sit down."

With the changes toward openness, Joanne added two reading chairs with a round coffee table in her office near the windows. She gestured that they move over there. "Tell me what's going on."

"I don't want to get into the details," Miles said. "I've been getting the sense that the expectation is that we are going to have to go into our childhood and bring up all of our crap. I don't want to do that. That's really uncomfortable for me. I don't share most of the things that happened in my childhood; it's not a place I want to go."

"Who told you that you have to do that?" asked Joanne.

"Everyone's aware of it," he shrugged.

"I don't understand this, Miles. I have been working with Mark and his team. The only time I go into anything childhood-related is when I choose to go there. When others have shared interesting experiences in conversation, it takes place because they always make sure that I'm comfortable with it. If I am, I am. If I'm not, I don't."

"That's not how it's being portrayed," Miles said. "And I'm not sure if you're telling me the truth."

"Miles, when is the last time I misled you?"

"I know you've been extremely truthful lately, but that hasn't been your track record. And someone says you are putting on a façade. You know the story of the devil, and the devil comes in light, but really underneath the light, it's the devil?"

Joanne stiffened. "What is this about?"

"I'm not so sure you are coming with pure intentions. What are your intentions, anyway?" Miles asked.

Joanne was taken aback; Miles had been her CFO for years. She knew she hadn't always been a great leader, but this seemed strange. "I want to see this company thrive," she said. "Mark presented an opportunity for us to move from losing money, being hateful and backstabbing, and underserving our customers, to a place where we are serving our customers exceptionally well, we are exceedingly profitable, and our company has become a happy place to work in. Isn't that enough?"

Miles had his arms folded—closed off. "That might be what you're telling everybody, but that is not the word in the company anymore."

"I've got to get to the bottom of this," Joanne said. "I *will* get to the bottom of this." She stood up and stepped toward the window.

Miles looked down at the dark coffee table. "I'll be gone in three weeks. Who do you want me to train?"

"You're not going anywhere," Joanne spun around, "until we get clear on what's happening."

"Three weeks," Miles said blandly. "I'm not playing anymore. I'm done." He got up. "I appreciate everything that you think the organization is going through to become. Maybe you thought it was all going to be roses. But you know what? There is a lot of pain."

"When did this start, Miles?" Joanne asked sympathetically.

"I started . . . I noticed it about six weeks ago."

"Six weeks, huh?" She remembered something; Amy had come into her office about six weeks ago and shared a story about her childhood. Amy began crying, saying the abuse had occurred from someone who was very close to her—how much betrayal she had experienced. She expressed fears that, somehow, everyone was going to find out. Amy wanted to protect herself, and looked to Joanne.

***

Miles was the first of three people to come to Joanne and give their resignation. She tried to have candid conversations with each of them, even others who worked with them, but each time she was given convoluted responses. Something strange was happening, and she couldn't put her finger on it. The souring situation seemed like more than the upheaval Mark had told her to expect. Joanne had begun to believe there was a revolt.

At one point, she came to work early as always, and there were a bunch of people outside the office.

"What's happening?" Joanne asked.

Amy stepped forward. "Joanne, we have an issue. We need the program to stop. You've got a revolt on your hands. I know you're aware of some of the stuff, but this isn't working. We have to stop the program. We have to move forward on our own. We're afraid that we are going to lose more and more of our employees. Word is starting to spread that some of the leaders are leaving, and it feels like we are on the *Titanic*. We are not sure if all of us are going to be able to stick with you. We have a serious challenge," Amy said, glancing back at all the people behind her. "You have to wake up and end this thing."

Joanne addressed the group, "Okay. If we choose as a company to end this, we want to make sure that we understand the truth of the situation and not the rumor mill that has been going about. I want to communicate with the entire company, and I want everyone to have a clear idea of why we are doing what we are doing, and we will see where people stand. In the end, I am going to make the final choice, but thank you for bringing this to my attention. I appreciate this information.

"Let's have a meeting today at one o'clock in the atrium. I'll meet with security, and ask that we have that space available. Jimmy, can you set up a microphone, and let's get some chairs down there?" Joanne looked around at all the anxious faces. "Anything else? Maybe we will get some snacks and drinks. Let's plan about a two-hour interaction with each other, okay?"

"Thank you, Joanne. Thank you, thank you," said someone at the back of the crowd.

CHAPTER TEN

THE CHOICE

My phone rang unusually early one morning.

"Mark," Joanne said. "I've got an issue. I'm not sure if we can continue."

"Okay," I said. "What's happening?"

Joanne explained the situation, and I had seen similar dynamics, but not to this degree. It's not uncommon when people start to change that their world begins to surface in ways that are different from their past patterns and expectations.

"Look," I said, "we don't know what is happening or why at this point. What we can count on is our training. Use the tools, and, as the leader, you have some choices to make."

Joanne sniffled. "But Mark," she said sadly, "I don't know if I am the leader for this. I don't know that I can bring the company through this. I've got some of my best people giving me their resignations."

"Are they still there?" Mark asked.

"Yeah, I mean, Miles will be gone in another week and a half. I . . . it's . . ."

I could sense her holding her breath. "Remember your breathing, Joanne," I suggested. She finally inhaled. "Joanne, how old do you feel?"

She laughed a little, "About four years old."

"Joanne, with all the care in the world, I want you to know that your organization is something that is near and dear to my heart. Not only that, but you as a person, as a human being, are near and dear to my heart." I could hear her crying between big breaths of air.

With a huge sigh she said, "Mark, thank you. I feel like you truly know me and understand where I'm coming from." She paused. "It's . . . I've never experienced this. It's so simple, but so rare to have a friendly, loving relationship between two human beings. It's just a pure, joy—love. It's like you're seeing my soul, the true nature of what I am, even when I'm not quite able to see it in the moment."

She laughed a little. "You know when we met and talked for the first time, I suddenly had a tinge of discomfort about my strategy. Here it was, out in the open, and here was someone who knew what I was trying to do. And you were willing just to share."

I smiled. "Joanne, every time you have been in a situation where things got hard, what was it that you did?"

"You know what? I would hide."

"Where would you hide?" I asked.

"A closet, a bedroom, a basement—I'd go where people weren't."

I could hear the tissue wipe across her face.

"Okay, so you separated yourself from the people who cared about you the most?"

"Yeah, I guess so," she sniffed. "That could be one way of looking at it."

"What would be another way of looking at it?"

"No, you're accurate." Joanne cleared her throat. "That's what I did. I tried to get away from people."

"Was there a favorite place that you liked to go?" I asked.

"Well, you know what I really liked?"

"What's that?"

"I liked going to a church." She gave a little chuckle. "A church. Really?"

"Not a church on a Sunday, but an empty one. When I was little, the church we went to had a little spot with stained glass windows—no other lights on. The sun would shine through them, and when I sat down and I just closed my eyes, it was almost like I was feeling the essence of God wrap around me and open me up and show me my goodness. It was beautiful."

"Was running away a way to get into that relationship?" I probed.

"Oh, absolutely!"

"What is your perception about running away?"

Joanne took a moment. "I think it's . . ." And she caught herself. "Wow, I guess I thought it was a weakness."

"*Is* moving from a situation that doesn't feel good to a situation that feels really good a weakness?"

"No, putting it like that, it doesn't sound like one," Joanne said with a smile. "I guess maybe my perception was inaccurate."

"Are you willing to let that perception fall away?"

"Absolutely—oh goodness! Not only have I been judging myself, but I have been judging my team. Here they are, running. I thought they were running from something. Maybe they are trying to get back in touch with something!"

"If that's the case, what is it that you most wanted when you were running?"

"I wanted to find a place where I could be alone with my thoughts, feel joy, and be inspired."

"Where could people in your company go to do this, to be inspired?"

"Well, it would be cool to create a meditation room, a space that is quiet, kind of like the church I grew up in," she said.

"Do you have a space where you could do that?" I asked.

"Wait a minute," Joanne said. "Do you have a space like this in your company?"

"We have a few of them."

"Why didn't you suggest we build one?"

"When you started, Joanne, remember, you didn't have any money. You were trying to get through crisis. This wasn't a high priority. Now that you are in a different scenario, it is coming to the forefront. And, I recommend you share the idea with your team."

"You mean share the story of my four-year-old — of my child — of my running, and what I was running to?" I could hear her tapping a pen on her desk.

"Why not?"

"It's pretty personal," Joanne said, "but I guess I have done a few vulnerable things at this point."

"Joanne, if you could find a way to create some calm and peace in your organization, to let them know that it's normal to find that — "

"Well, here's the thing," Joanne said, interrupting. "It's not just about the space."

"Oh?" I asked.

"It seems that I have an employee who is potentially sabotaging the organization. I don't *know* with certainty if she is sabotaging or not, but we are at a point where a lot of people are divided. It appears that some want to move forward and through this, and keep the program, but some want to get rid of it. The people who want to get rid of it have a stronger voice right now than the people who are learning from it. It's still so new to everyone. They haven't experienced all the depths that I have, and I know more good is coming."

"Well," I said, "you know some of what is coming. It's a great adventure, and if you're willing to continue, it's going to be extraordinary. I know when you said you were 100 percent committed, you didn't anticipate this mess. If you want to get away from it and run, I would encourage you to go to that church—go away and take a weekend. Think about this. Tune into the very essence of who it is you are and your relationship with your Creator. See what is really best for the organization. Choose from that space of calm, peace, and love.

"The space of anxiety that you are in and the worry about where people are going to land, that is going to create a negative or destructive outcome. That is the emotional space from which you were making choices before. Remember, you have been making more and more choices from the space of pure love. If you can stay and maintain that love while you are thinking about this, and all the people, including this person you think might be sabotaging this organization, you might be surprised how brilliantly your guidance system will come alive—how you will know exactly what to do and when to do it.

"By yourself, you would never be able to navigate through this. It's about a surrendering, an allowance, a letting go of what you thought needed to be done, your old patterns of reaction, and stepping into allowing for something new, something that can build on the past yet be present right now."

She took a sigh and breathed and said, "You know what? I called a meeting this afternoon. I think your insight is sound, though."

"Okay, when is the meeting?"

"It's going to be a few hours from now."

"Okay," I said. "What is your inclination as to what to do?"

"I think I am going to go out into nature. It's another spot where I can immerse myself, surrender, and find inspiration."

"Wonderful!" I said. "It's a place where I also get inspiration."

"There's a path in the woods near the office," Joanne shared. "It's totally enclosed. Even though there are buildings hidden by the forest, from underneath the tree canopy, I feel as if I am in wonderland."

CHAPTER ELEVEN

WALKING THE WALK

When Joanne hung up the phone, she went out to the woods and started to ask who it is that she needed to be as a leader. The answers became extremely uncomfortable. She began to see the leaders of the past, and some of them she thought were really angry and ugly and didn't make good choices. Many of her mentors and teachers she grew up with had led to her dysfunction. She also saw leaders that were wonderful, loving, expressive, and just awesome— courageous leaders. She saw the split, the division in her of seeing the strengths in one or the other, and which one she was. She suggested to herself through this spiritual walk that maybe it was time to let go of all the *pleasing* in her idea of leadership, to release the definitions of being a leader, and come face-to-face with who she was as a human being.

It took about forty-five minutes, but at the end of the forty-five minutes, she had a whole speech. It was as if someone had downloaded it within her, and it was just there. She didn't speak a word of it; she just knew she had it. Inside herself, she got the green light: *I'm ready.*

Joanne walked back to the office and completed a few tasks. No stress. Didn't do any preparation other than what she had done on the walk. She entered the atrium at one o'clock, and the entire company was pouring in. She loved the atrium because there was nature in the atrium. Once everyone arrived, Joanne asked them to do three things before they began.

She said, "Look around and see the beauty of the plants in here." It wasn't an atrium where there were one or two trees; it was really like a mini-forest. It was a lushly green, beautiful place. "Look around and find the thing that you consider to be the most beautiful. When you have it, begin to just breathe and relax," Joanne said, giving everyone a moment to focus.

She took a deep breath, herself, and began, "We are in a state of aggression in this company. I have heard stories about people who are truly harming each other. The principles that we have been learning from Rookha Group, we are not fully practicing. I know some are doing better than others and a few are not participating.

"Additionally, it appears that we may have a saboteur among us. Perhaps it's us. Perhaps we're aware of it, and we are doing it intentionally. Perhaps it's happening but we're not even aware of it.

"As you notice this beauty around us, and take in this breath, I'd like you to think about three things during our conversation. The first: Who is it that you are? Not who is it that you are in your work. role, and not who is it that you are as a parent, or a sibling, or anything like that, but roles aside, who is it that you truly are, the being-ness of you? I'd like you to remember some of the early teachings that the Rookha Group talked about, and how you tuned in to that. Remember who it is you are."

Joanne paused for a few seconds. "The second thing: I'd like you to recall the way that I was about four years ago, and the way that I was about six months ago, and the way that I am today. Me, personally— *Joanne,* your CEO." Some chuckles and smiles went around the room.

Some of them had been in the company a long time. She knew they saw her as insecure four years ago, and were not sure if she was ripe to become a CEO. Joanne had felt confused and conflicted, never really being comfortable in that role. Six months ago, she was frustrated and angry and scared that what they built was going to fall and crumble. And now, Joanne was a confident and courageous CEO—loving and nurturing and seeing each person for who they were and not the objects she had seen them as six months earlier. This was apparent to everyone in the room who had been there in any of those transitions.

"And the third thing," she said. "I want to know if you are willing to come into the future with me, to step forward into the future where I believe we're headed. And that future is going to be the next six minutes."

For six minutes, Joanne described her vision of what the company was becoming—a vision now present in her after much work and quietly listening to that refined inner guidance system. These goals were what she had really wanted from the beginning, and didn't know how to see. But now, the path was being revealed.

"They weren't giving us a prescriptive path," Joanne said to her people, "but what Rookha Group was giving us were the right tools so we could discover our own path. We can discover our own paths as individuals, and the path of our organization, and within that, the groups, the teams, the collaboration, and the celebration of success."

The thing she closed with was on the projector behind her: Their numbers. "This is a picture of our financials six months ago. It was a disaster. Take note of the red all over the slide." Joanne heard gasps from everyone who had been kept in the dark at the time. "This was our bank account," and they looked shocked. "This was our payroll, by the way," and she showed it. Their payroll was way higher than their bank account.

"And now, I am going to show you our numbers today." The next slide was all black. "Profits. The bank account has built to a level that is still growing, but far healthier than where it was before. Our line of credit has been paid down quite a bit, cut in half. We have become a healthy organization, and we're getting healthier by the day.

"When Mark first introduced this program to me, he said that it was going to be a tough transition; that this wasn't going to be all roses. Yet, the definite purpose of this program is that we have to be a light to our customer base and a light to employees, so that we attract and retain the very best people." Joanne looked around the atrium until she saw Miles and Amy, sitting together in front but off to the left.

"One of the things that this transformation requires is for each of us to look within ourselves. You need to determine if you want to be here or not. You have challenged me as to whether this program should stay or go." Joanne looked right at Miles and Amy. "The program, as it stands, stays."

"No," Amy said under her breath. "Damn it all." She looked at Miles, "Fuck."

Joanne continued to address the room, confidently, "And, if you have heard rumors of anything that is out of integrity with the vision that I shared—that we can step fully into and became an optimal organization, just as the Rookha Group has been mentoring us—then I encourage you, no matter what your role is in this organization, to first go to your direct leader and address it head on. Call us out. If our words or our actions are not in integrity, call us out. I encourage you, if you don't get satisfaction from your leader, to come together with your leader, go to your next leader, or come to me directly. I encourage you all, within a twenty-four-hour period, to get satisfaction to your concerns. Be in a position where you are dealing with the actuality of the situation, and not the issues that might be resonated by someone else who is putting out information that could be false.

"Tell you what," and Joanne pointed right to Amy. "Let's say I went to Amy and I told Amy, 'Hey, Joanne is really lying to everybody, and she is not truly trying to do what she says we're trying to do.' You feel very uncomfortable about that, Amy, but instead of addressing it, you start living from that new question. That choice can create a ripple effect."

Then Joanne pointed to Miles, "Let's say Amy then goes out and meets with Miles, and they have a conversation. Suddenly, Miles is influenced."

Amy and Miles looked at each other with a look of *how does she know?* on their faces.

"Did you tell?" Amy mouthed to Miles.

"No, I didn't tell," he leaned in to whisper back.

"How does she . . ." Amy stopped herself and looked at Joanne. "What . . . what's going on here?" Amy looked back at Miles and said, "We gotta get out of here. I am really uncomfortable. I gotta go." Amy cast her eyes to the floor and walked to the back of the atrium.

Miles stayed in his seat, wide-eyed as she left.

Joanne watched this unfolding, and then continued, "That kind of thing is stopping today. So, let's dispel these rumors that have been going around."

By the end of the meeting, nearly everyone in attendance left feeling comfortable, knowing where she and the company stood, and that they all had choices to make: would they stay and grow? Or, would they go?

***

On the way out, Joanne sent a text to reach out to Amy. "Meet me in my office. Joanne."

Joanne figured Amy didn't want to meet, but was pleased when she came. Joanne sat her down and said, "Is there something you want to tell me?"

Amy looked down at the carpet. "Joanne, I'm sorry. I'm scared. I did say a few things. I didn't want the program. I don't want it."

"I understand," Joanne said. "But I am going to encourage you to leave with dignity."

"What?" Amy said, big-eyed.

"I am going to encourage you to leave with dignity."

"You're firing me?"

"No. It's clear that it's not a fit, though. People who stay here, I want them to see that this organization's vision can be realized. As far as I can tell, it seems that you have been culpable of putting out misinformation. Intentional or not, it's okay. But you're not a fan of our plan. When you're ready, if you'd ever like to come back, I would welcome you with open arms. But it would be on your availability to enter into a situation that allows for you to be the very best person you can be. Where are you right now, it doesn't appear that this is the place for you."

Amy cried a few tears and said, "You know, I've never been fired before. I'm not even sure if I'm being fired. But if ever I were to fire someone, this is a really nice way to do it." She let out a big sigh. "I feel like you are doing what's in my best interest."

"I am."

CHAPTER TWELVE

TURNOVER

Over the course of the following month, Joanne and her leadership team met with all the employees, and every one of them made a choice. A few chose to leave, and they left on great terms. My team and I worked with them, and they created a phenomenal execution plan to support people in moving into new jobs.

Amy left, and she and Miles broke off their relationship. Miles apologized for his role, and he chose to stay. He got some additional support to release the judgment he had about his acting against the company. Miles was ready to transition into a place where he began to lead effectively. Although he had made some poor choices, those choices were explored, learned from, and all agreed, after an emotionally releasing discussion, to move forward.

Miles was now in a position where he could mentor others with the very thing he was most uncomfortable with. All his life, Miles put himself in the position to please others in his relationships. But it wasn't constructive to be in a place where he was pleasing his girlfriend, mom, dad, or his boss. That was not optimal. Neither he or the organization would enable it anymore. So, Miles became a teacher on that particular topic. Initially, Miles was supported by some of the Rookha team members, but then he was doing it on his own and becoming a support leader for the program.

Miles became an advocate at such a high level that many new employees were coming over to Rookha Group from his network. These new employees came because, after working with Miles, they looked for a company that engaged the full human being and wouldn't just hire them for their skill, or for their definitive need of a job. Miles hired people for their desire to be a part of something bigger than themselves, to impact lives, and to grow.

Every single person who would work with Miles had on their resume some inkling to want to further develop, not rest where they were, but had a desire to get to the next level with a team. The people who came in and went through the enrollment process as new members of the team were brilliant. Teams began to grow, and the individuals performed as individuals. Many stayed much longer than the average tenured employee. When people did leave, it was because their heart awakened in them something new that pulled them in a different direction.

Joanne's company performed nicely. They communicated in the way they were taught when Rookha Group came in.

Everyone who came in the door was told, "At some point, you might want to leave. We will celebrate when you come, and we will celebrate when you go. It's your life. When you join our company as a member of this team, it's for however long you'd like to be here and we'd like you to stay. It will be a joint choice. We will work with you. We will provide the tools for all of our employees to support their well-being, and we will bring the very best in this organization to our communities and to the people we serve."

CHAPTER THIRTEEN

MERGER

It was a Saturday, and Joanne and I met together for breakfast. I was so excited to meet with her that I arrived twenty minutes early. As Joanne sat down and our breakfast arrived, I reached across the table with a notebook, and said, "Look, you have done so many amazing things with your company. It's been a few years since we began working with you. I'm so impressed with what you've done. It's because of you and your team that you are in the position you're in. I have a vision that I want to share with you, and I'd like to walk you through this."

She got a little bit perplexed, as I was pointing to the notebook. It read, *The Merger*. She looked up at me and said, "What?"

I said, "Listen, I have a vision that was created. My team has done a great job coming up with it. But it's a ten-year vision. It will require a lot of work. Now Joanne, I'd like to be moving toward some of the dreams that Liz and I have to travel and serve in another way. I'd like you to look at this and just consider it.

"We have had this global expansion underway. But I'd like to take it to the next level. We started looking around at companies that would be good fits. Obviously, with Breaha and you doing such a marvelous job, our team kept bringing you up. Your transformation has been so miraculous and wonderful, and your team is solid. We are so well aligned."

"Yes, we are," Joanne said with a smile. "Ever since Breaha took over presidential duties, she has mentioned this as a vision she has. She thinks it is why she left for our firm in the first place — to help us be ready for this merger. Brilliant!"

"I have an idea that we join together and build the vision that is laid out here. Of course, you can add your input. But, if this is where I am at today, and if it sounds similar to where you want to go, let's join together and make this a reality."

Joanne lifted her glass of orange juice. "Cheers to our friendship!" Then with a casual bite of eggs Benedict, she started to look through the vision. "Hmm, there are things I haven't actually considered before, but it's resonating with me. I think it's something I would be excited about." She got to the end and said, "Well, Mark, what would it look like?"

"I'm thinking that we would need a leader who gets this work," I said.

"Uh huh?" she said cheekily.

"We would need someone who is young enough to carry out the ten-year vision and passionate enough in the vision to hold true to it, to bring it about, who can see it already realized and step fully in there with me and my team."

"I'm your gal," Joanne said with a wink.

"I know," I said.

"Maybe," Joanne said, "We could bring our two companies together for a joint picnic and announce then?"

I smiled. "I like that. It would be a scenario where they got to have fun together. We could play all kinds of fun collaborative games."

Joanne was almost giddy. "And we could mix the teams up so there will be some from each company on each team! This will be great!"

***

The day for the picnic rolled around, and everyone at first thought it was simply a celebratory event. Yet, it was not lost on anyone that they had never done this before and there was a strong alignment between the companies. Rumors of a possible merger had already sprinkled through the congregation of people by lunchtime.

As the day went on with softball games, volleyball, pony rides, and trampolines, Joanne and I made an announcement to gather in the meadow. We set up on the grass where people could bring blankets. Hundreds of people sprawled out in the sunshine. There was a stage in front with microphones and speakers along the sides, so everyone could hear.

Joanne and her leadership team went to one side of the stage, and my leadership team and I were at the other. At first, we celebrated the winners of the events and gave out prizes and awards. One of the most fun awards was for the bag-turning tournament grand prize winners. It was a tie. People were chuckling and celebrating as we replayed Sean's reverse behind-the-back throw for the win — a-never-been-seen-before move in bag-turn history, at least in this crowd. His five-hundred-dollar gift certificate to the restaurant The Waxing Moon drew jeers like *Hey, you're taking me, right?* and some chuckling and joking around. It was a fun, festive, joyous time.

When Joanne took the stage and began to speak, even before anyone had said the word *merger*, it was as if the entire group had known that it was going to happen. She started to thank Rookha Group for all the things they had brought into her organization, and how without the tools that they had brought forth, she didn't know where the company would be now. But she was quite certain it wouldn't be where it was today.

In that expression of gratitude, Joanne turned to me, and I started to share my joy about how well customers were receiving both companies' offerings around the globe. Our company had about seven times more employees than Joanne's company, but I was quick to recognize our shared vision and thought that it would be a good moment to announce jointly that we were going to merge.

We began to share how the details would work, starting with a six-month period where the two companies could simply try it. They would come together with the intention of fully executing the merger within that time, but start operating immediately as if it had already been happening. Each person would be scheduled for a meeting so that any concerns they had would be addressed. Joanne shared that there were plenty of jobs. The vision was going to allow for people to either stay and remain in their role, or have opportunities to move to other roles in the expansion as it was happening.

There was a whoop and a holler from everyone on the meadow, and a huge celebration commenced with champagne and cake. Joanne and I had successfully created an environment where, even in the midst of uncertainty, the whole population of people knew how to handle an experience of uncertainty and to step fully into it. Most companies that have gone through migrations, changes, and mergers experience a lot of anxiety. The anxiety at the picnic, if there was any, was subtle. If it came up, each person had the tools to release it. In fact, not only did each employee have those tools, but they had expanded these programs to allow their families to come in. Many of the family members had been through the program as well.

One of the most enjoyable things for Joanne and me that day was seeing how welcome and receptive people were to the idea of a merger. We capped off the huge celebration with fireworks that shot off from behind the stage. It was one of those special, surreal moments in my life. Music started to play, the fireworks went off; nightfall had subtly come in so the fireworks could be seen, but the sun was still on the horizon line. The pink sky just starting to fade into darkness — it was a beautiful, touching moment — one I was sure we would all remember for a long time to come.

EPILOGUE

Your Optimal Leader is awaiting you to lay down anything blocking the full expression of it on a consistent basis. As you do, you can more easily create a culture that supports others doing the same, living as the very essence of themselves, Love, Life, their *Optimal Being*. When people do this their minds become clear, their hearts become pure, and they find more joy and fulfillment in life, including relationships, interests, and careers. Along the way their abilities sharpen and new ones appear.

We believe within every organization exists an optimal workforce; one aligned and engaged as optimal beings joining together for a common mission.

Explore this by reading The Awakened Workforce (also by Mark Hattas and the Rookha Group team). This book focuses on the ten elements of well-being, colorfully illustrated via stories shared by ten individuals working for the "Easy Breezy" company. Each highlights their experience with an element of well-being that had challenged them the most.

The stories have been fictionalized, yet the

transformations are real. You might even find a bit of you in the characters. A summary of the 10 elements of well-being can be found for free at optimalbeing.live/elements, which also has a link to purchase the book.

Learn to live as an Optimal Being today!!

Mark and Team

ABOUT THE AUTHOR

Mark Hattas, Cofounder, Rookha Group, Inc.

Mark is an excellent coach and leader. He helps people get clear on optimal next steps rapidly. Even the most accomplished leaders progress to their next level with Mark. Through programs like Optimal Being® he and his team members can benefit your entire organization.

He began his career at GE Medical/Healthcare before starting, building and selling Geneca, a tech firm, over a twelve-year period. At sale, they had grown to nearly 150 team members and $20M in revenue.

Mark and his team are exceptional at helping leaders realize their vision and enjoy the journey.

Additionally, Mark co-founded Journey's Dream (journeysdream.org, *501c3*), a support hub for hope and restored mental/emotional wellness.

He is an internationally best-selling author in *Journeys to Success: Health, Wellness, and Fitness Edition*, and author of *"IT": A Children's Book about Encouragement and Discovering One's Gifts*.

Mark also co-founded Discover Ancient Wisdom, LLC and has contributed to the Boards of i.c.stars and Charles Tillman's Cornerstone Foundation.

Mark is sharing the adventure of life with his wonderful wife, Liz, and their five much loved children. He is grateful and experiences life as a blessing.

Find out more, including free resources, stories, and pillars of health information at markhattas.com.

Explore more at optimalbeing.live, and discover products and services supporting Awakening the Optimal Leader in you and others in your organization.